D1785355

THE TOOTH IS THE LARGEST ORGAN IN THE HUMAN BODY

HOLLY DAY

ANAPHORA LITERARY PRESS

QUANAH, TEXAS

ANAPHORA LITERARY PRESS
1108 W 3rd Street
Quanah, TX 79252
https://anaphoraliterary.com

Book design by Anna Faktorovich, Ph.D.

Copyright © 2020 by Holly Day

All rights reserved. No part of this book may be reproduced in any form or by any electronic or mechanical means, including information storage and retrieval systems, without permission in writing from Holly Day. Writers are welcome to quote brief passages in their critical studies, as American copyright law dictates.

Printed in the United States of America, United Kingdom and in Australia on acid-free paper.

Published in 2020 by Anaphora Literary Press

The Tooth Is the Largest Organ in the Human Body
Holly Day—1st edition.

Library of Congress Control Number: 2020903777

Library Cataloging Information
Holly, Day, 1971-, author.
    The Tooth Is the Largest Organ in the Human Body / Holly Day
    94 p. ; 9 in.
    ISBN 978-1-68114-529-7 (softcover : alk. paper)
    ISBN 978-1-68114-530-3 (hardcover : alk. paper)
    ISBN 978-1-68114-531-0 (e-book)
1. Poetry—Women Authors. 2. Poetry—American—General.
3. Poetry—Subjects & Themes—Nature.
PN6099-6110: Collections of general literature: Poetry
811: American poetry in English

CONTENTS

Just Ending

there's something comforting about
the temporary nature of poetry
that once the words are written
your work is done

there's no need to labor to match words
to music, to craft lyrics that need
to be paced to a danceable beat
there's no need to balance color
against canvas, prepare wooden frames
to wrap the painting around
mix tincture

and with a poem
you just turn the page
and it's gone

These Things

My husband says he hates this house
And its rough edges
And the bad memories
I don't know what he's talking about.

At dinner, I give pointed lectures to our daughter
About how you get from life what you put into it
How if you think the world is shit, your world will be shit.
My husband doesn't seem to know I'm talking to him
And tells our daughter maybe she should smile every once in a while
Not be such a sourpuss.

My husband says he hates this life
Doesn't know what he did to deserve
A wife like me
A family like ours
A house like this
I tell him he must have really fucked up in his last life
This is the shit-end of karma.

Springtime in Minnesota

homeless
emerge from their cocoons

of newspapers
and army blankets, pour out
of automobiles closed tight
against winter, shake

potato chip crumbs off of clothes
that don't rot in the negative degrees
spread arms to the sky, hands

blossoming for change

Anonymous and Cool

slow leak, I'm running out of air
here, you are a deep blue ocean
I should have stayed out of, spending
too much time trying to patch up things
when I should have been running away

I would give anything to be able to stare into your eyes
dead-on and say, "I love you"
and mean it

put your fingers back on me, the one place
left unblemished—I used to say the words
each day
and now I don't know what they mean
all this thinking
of what might have been.

Mackerel

fish, all kinds
speak to me
from the streets
calling out loudly
as I pass
the merchants with their

ice-packed carts
and primitive refrigeration units

the newspaper
tells me
this is supposed to be
a sign from God

but no one
will tell me
what kind of sign
or what
I should do.

Nothing

The man on TV claims he is not responsible
for my remolding, that these images

of hygienic solvents, naked children wrapped
in bathroom tissue, sweaters and pants

that dance all on their own
are just figments of my own hard drive

imagination. Lies to me. These are not my visions
fingernails drag by, whisper

the barest of truths—
sometimes, he sounds

just like you.

Hudson

The lawnmower makes me wish
I was an animal, some four-footed hoofed thing
that lives on flowers and tree bark.
Its noise makes me run and
hide in my room.

These clothes make me wish
I was pure beast, a sleeked-furred creature
that gave birth in a den
fed carrion to my children.
These clothes make me ugly and
keep me meek.

This bed makes me wish
I was alone, or something with claws
that I had my own scent, and not that of the man
that lumbers in here at night
and says that I'm his.

That Place

knuckle deep in the slot Dad kicked when
he found out. hurts. dream of angels
wake to red sheets telephone
too far away

knuckle deep in the slot meant to fill,
he said, finger lickin' lyin' cheat
swore to be there protect me hold me
gone minutes seconds after pulling out
too late

knuckle deep in the slot the cocoon burst from,
butterfly folded up still, quiet, black eye
sightless squirrel paws praying wings unformed
too early to tell to name to beg forgiveness
holding legs tight together fingers trying
to stop the flood

Gerontophobia

I don't need you to
short-change my fuck-
hole, old man—your
limp cold against my
tongue makes me sick,
makes me as wrinkled
and puckered as your
wife is soft and
stretches like a Slinky
poised to creep down
the staircase of your
antiseptic house

Heat

I feel the carnivore inside me dying
I need meat, I need you.
Don't let me down.

Take away these melodramatic dreams of blood
let's play master and child,
predator and wife, man and prey.
Don't ever leave.

Floor Pie

when dreams of escape fade
into wasted breath
she picks up her memories

like cloudy marbles
whispers
"this is what pockets are for"

those men in the hall
are like needles

that shouldn't be used again

Table of Contents

I want to write about the sun coming
up over the emptiness of the ocean,
unbroken save for waves or maybe even
an abandoned oil derrick—I want to write
about wide open spaces. I close my eyes
and can almost see the way it looks when you
stand on top of a mountain on a clear day
and can see all the way to Catalina
Island—almost, but not quite.

City streets crowd out my words,
the crazy old lady down
the street that had her entire
lawn paved over, the boy next door
who likes to kill stray cats. The stars
die before they're even born in
my mind, blotted out by stadium
floodlamps and sickly yellow crime lights,
the mountains crumble as cars drive
over them and trains rumble through them.

I want to write about the beaches
of San Juan before the Spanish landed,
the way Louisiana looked the first time
white men rowed down the Mississippi
and into the Bay—I want to write about
the smell of sulfur after a lightning storm,
the way the wind sounds when it blows
miniature tornadoes through
the Arizona desert, but my head's too full
of traffic lights and city noise
to begin to form the words.

Bleeding For

you drive me to church
silent lip-synch choir "hail mary's"
fingers fasten on the hem of my dress
keep it down

you drive me to prayer
revelations screamed to a god never known
force my hands from doing things
it will be you

you are in me always
bright ideal to offer psalms up to
totem dream to blame my pain on
come to me

Fred, Half Dead, Beethoven In His Head

You can't talk to Beethoven
on a bus stop in Chicago
because you'll just get lost.

Lauded as a genius,
he can't give good directions
because he's dead.
.

Ask Fred about Beethoven
about Fred
his hands will wave wildly with excitement like
the vibrations coming up through his feet.
conducting symphonies in an empty room.

Fred will tell you how planets hum
give directions to angry flocks of pigeons
lecture on string theory
like harpsichords, and how Beethoven was more
of a transcriber than a composer.

I picture the two sitting together
lost in deep conversation.

First/Last Page

flames darken the single sheet of paper
some words burn brighter than the rest
typewriter lies dead in the corner
angry teeth inlaid with rusted iron bits

typewriter burns bright in the corner
on the floor, keyboard split, askew
carefully-set pieces of ebony screaming
a mouthful of flames darkening the neatly-typed words.

They Come at Night

I know how to read men even
with my eyes closed, hands out, fingers reading
the Braille of sweat, of the man on the bed
beside me. I pretend I'm deaf

so he won't talk to me, but I have been alive just long enough
to know when someone is about to come
even through
the soles of my feet, to know exactly
the conclusion of invisible things. If this man

wants to talk to me
afterwards, hold me in his cool, strong arms
whisper muddled endearments into my ears
that's fine, so long as he doesn't expect a response.
In the morning, I'll tell him
about how even songbirds sound suspicious
when you've had your heart broken.

When We First

he gave me the new word, "love"
folded it into fourths, tore it to careful pieces of pink confetti.
I swallowed hard, felt it go down my throat

and although the pieces were so tiny, so small
I could still feel them somewhere inside me,
halfway down, lodged and refusing to move.

I got the second word, "home," shortly afterward
the individual letters were illegible, as though someone else
had tried to swallow them before me
could only be reassembled through the process of

imagination. Some of the pieces of this new
disassembled puzzle
must have gotten stuck on their way down,
because although I do believe the words are still there, inside me
something in me still doesn't understand what they mean.

Like Snakes on Asphalt

My father's horizon was always
Nebraska, he never grew past being
a tiny spot surrounded by miles
of cattle-flattened silage
stunted sagebrush.

I don't know the names of either
of my horizons, can only guess
at who lives in the row of dark houses
across the street. I am also

an unnecessary pinpoint
surrounded by flat, black asphalt
waves of heat radiating from
crumbling tar.

And Only Infrequently

We exchange pictures through the mail because words
aren't good enough. The passage of time is explained
through the faces of strangers, in the pictures of children
only known in person as tiny, warm babies
coiled and asleep, newly born. The envelopes

also contain pictures of people I know
but older, grayer, tired. My sister's gap-toothed smile
has been replaced by the tight grin
of a woman with perfect teeth
standing next to her own family—her goofy college sweetheart
is now a man holding hands with a toddler.
I put pictures of me, my children, their father
in a similar envelope
seal it without looking

without wanting to look
still in denial that time
has passed at this end as well.

The Poet

The ship crashes against the rocks and a poem
Forms in her head right as she flies over the railing
Something so perfect and beautiful it must be written down
Must be remembered. She invokes the first stanza

For the otters watching curiously from the rocks,
The seals lounging carelessly on the beach
The dolphins she knows must be lurking just past the shallows
Because there are always dolphins watching shipwrecks
And dolphins are smart and literate enough to understand poetry.

She shouts the lines as clearly as she can
Despite the screaming of the other passengers
Despite the rending, grinding agony of the hull against the rocks
Despite the shrieks of the confused seagulls whirling overhead
Because she knows this is a poem that cannot be lost
And somebody has to be left behind to remember.

The River Otter

The otter sleeps in the river, wrapped
in duckweed and watercress, tiny paws folded
over its chest. I resign myself to stretching out
in the sun-warmed shallows, hands spread out in the water
determined to catch vestiges of the river otter's dreams.

In fairy tales, this would be the time when the river otter
would wake and swim out to me to speak
of wishes and promises and secret treasures and marriage
emerge a prince from the water, dripping jewels and starlight
instead, tiny, unbidden ripples
spread across the water from where I lay
to where the otter sleeps, don't, won't stop

until the animal wakes and swims away.

Jaybird

from the other end of the line
you calmly deliver me
of my dreams of a real family
of a future with you.

how easy it is for you
to sever these bonds between us
how easy it is
for you to cut me free

while I am still hanging on edge
remembering you asleep beside me
how much I still love you.

Whisper to a Mason Jar

I'm in love with the little midges
that dance in the sunlight, their green wings
fluttering so quickly that they seem suspended in mid-air.
When I die, I want to become a creature like that
cavorting in sunbeams and buffeted by the wind.

I love the little spiders, too, tiny, bright
transparent and gelatinous but full of so much potential.
Just to know that I could grow from a pinprick
a spot on a piece of paper
into a hairy brute that sent housewives screaming
to the top of chairs, a bird-killer,
something with venom powerful enough
to stop a man's heart
I could wind my dreams around that.

I love the fireflies the best, though
blinking serenades across the water
disguising themselves as perfectly ordinary brown beetles
only unfurling their secret starlight at night.
I am also a firefly. I know
there is potential for sunshine inside me as well,
there is an unexpected brilliance
just waiting to explode.

Downstream

the dying cricket tries to sing but its wings
are too wet to make a sound. It struggles to reach
the edge of a furled bay leaf also caught in the swift-moving current
but the leaf is carried away too fast for the cricket to reach.

Overhead, tiny gnats dip and glide just above the surface
of the water, they follow the cricket's tiny body
all the way downstream where it's washed up on shore
crumpled and dead and safe to bury eggs in. The sun

will eventually dry the thin, black wings and legs, the wind
will push and pull at the cricket's hollow remains and make
these sad little parts
sing one last time.

Bloodlines

The maple sends its helicopter seeds across the yard
in desperate dreams of propagation. I rake most of them up
rip out the long roots of the ones that slip past me
take root and try to grow. I sometimes wonder
if my tree hates me, if it feels angry when it sees me

with my gardening shears clipping its offspring close to the ground
or if it's resigned itself to the fact that it will never be surrounded
by a forest of its own family. I think of these violent acts of mine
during heavy storms when the limbs of the tree whips around my roof

if it's using the wind and the lightning as an excuse to drop branches
and clumps of leaves on my lawn, if it's aiming for me and my chil-
dren
in an act of retaliation so sly it won't ever be blamed.

To End in Tragedy

the octopi approach one another with resignation
knowing their coupling is doomed
that there is no happy end to this story.
Their limbs float around them as they hesitantly
embrace, as if not sure when or whose caresses
will turn violent, as if hoping that, if they just take it slow,
they can enjoy this
for more than a short, stolen moment of happiness.

The Ditch

The day my great-granddad died, he dug the hole
by himself, all the way square to six feet deep.
Jumped in the hole, lay down
pulled his gun out and
shot himself clean through the head.
His suicide note just said
"Shouldn't be too much trouble
just push the dirt back in."

Apparently inspired by this story,
my grandmother's first husband
hung himself in the bedroom he shared
with his wife, left the door wide open
so anyone coming into the house would first see
his shit and piss-stained body dangling from the ceiling.
My aunt and uncle, aged 5 and 7, found this waiting
when they came home from school.

When my husband talks about suicide
I tell him
make it clean.

Hot Sunshine Song

I tried to open my heart to you
felt the petals stick as they struggled
like the warped bud of a sick tulip—fungal
at the root, I tried
to love you but I didn't know how.

You tried to help me, I think
armed with harpoons and bone snares that
meant love, but only the jagged edges
registered anything with me.
I forget the good things I know were there.

We could have been good together
if the right pieces had met at the right time,
instead of crashing like icebergs,
breaking into cold snow.

Time Capsule

Our history has already degraded
to the rubber soles of a pair of shoes
and an ivory thimble.
Nobody will be able to read

the newspapers
destroyed by years of rainwater
leaking in through the cracks
freezing solid every winter, no one

will be able to read the rolled-up scroll
placed ceremoniously in the box
announcing that day's events
the photographs of our town
doomed to quick decay through faulty design.

The Spaces Between

I show my house the pictures of you
ask it if it remembers when you lived closer
when you were a frequent guest. I feel the ache and the strain
of a house trying to uproot itself, as if
it was some great, lazy dog trying to find the will to move
twitching its tail in a futile attempt
to attract attention to itself.

I, too, wish I could find some way to reach you
that doesn't require the enormous effort it takes to get to the airport
or make plans that involve weeks and weeks of my life in advance.
These are fragile excuses, ones
I don't dare speak aloud. Instead, I tell the house

you'll be back someday
to sit on my couch and fill these empty rooms
with your stories and your laughter
and it will be so wonderful that it will be as if
you'd never left.

Trying to Be

As the years pass, I have grown more aware
of all of the things I seem unable to write about:
love, for one thing. I don't know how
to write anything convincing about love.

As my children grow up and my husband gets older
I grow more and more resigned to the things I can't feel:
love, especially, I don't think I know what it is.
If I sit and analyze my heart
I'm uncomfortably aware of this pantomime of caring
my fake day-to-day. This is something

I can write about:
my shortcomings as a human.
The things I haven't done.
All of my lies.

(A)

Sometimes when you're too rough I'm afraid
you're trying to kill me, but then I don't know
if I mind. I don't know how I want to die, which specific way
I would pick if offered a selection of possible calamities
but I suspect

that if being suffocated against your chest
as you crested, oblivious to my flailing fists
my squeals of indignation
my inevitable silence, the suspicious stillness
was one of the choices on that hypothetical list
it would probably be up there in my top ten choices.

When You Want Me Least

You, who are so different, can't be
expected to agree on anything
with me. I just need you to hold me long enough
to understand what is written on the small tag attached
to my toe, and then you can go.

There are streamers and iridescent ribbons
for you to reflect on
while you sit here with me, in the dark
a newspaper with your name written in black felt pen
over the original headlines
memories of what we could have had
if you had only become the president, or the Pope.

The real memories
are still here, somewhere, as well as
the rest of my heart. You
can wrap them all to go
if you want to forget.

Anticipation

It's gotten to the point
where if I don't see or speak to someone
for a certain length of time
I just assume they're dead.
If my neighbor doesn't come out
to shovel the snow off her of her sidewalk by the end of the day

I instantly picture
her lying on the floor of her bathroom,
blood pooling by a large gash on her head,
perhaps a bottle of heart medication
lying on the floor, just out of reach
of her pale, outstretched fingers.

I call my parents more than I used to
answer the phone every time my mother calls
convinced
that it can only be bad news.
It's gotten to the point

that every muscle cramp, every headache
makes me think of cancer, I am
just waiting for that last
shoe to drop.

Friday

The flies settle around me as if preparing for congress
and I, I pretend I am one of them, I am also a fly.
We converse about the habits of frogs and the placement of eggs
and what it would be like to be a cat or a dog.

We talk until sundown, until they fly off
to sleep in those secret places only real flies know about
and I go back in to pretend at humanity
listen to my mom as she talks about my dad.

Motes of Sparkling Glass

You can teach brine shrimp to dance
by shining a flashlight into their tank
and moving it back and forth. They will follow the light
like a scarf of sparkling dust mites
like a swarm of swallows alighting for the night
like a cloud of gnats discovering a piece of rotted fruit
like a pulse of transparent blood vessels traveling along a vein.

What they don't tell you
in the manual that comes with the tank
that says shining a light into the tank will teach them to dance
is that you're really just tricking the tiny shrimp into thinking
that their hiding place been suddenly exposed to sunlight
and sometimes it kills them
and sometimes it forces them to change sex
and sometimes it makes them spontaneously reproduce
and sometimes it does nothing at all, because this whole time
the tiny specks of dust you shook into the water of your sea monkey
      tank

weren't actually brine shrimp eggs at all
but just bits of sand gathered from the shore of some faraway beach,
some beautiful, warm, tropical place
that you will never get to see for yourself.

The Dog

My mother-in-law brought the dog home the day after I brought my
      baby home.
The thing was huge, a great big standard poodle, fully grown with
      black eyes
nearly covered in thick curly brown fur. It never made a sound, just
      watched everyone
moving around the house, every once in a while asking to be let out
      the back door.

The dog didn't react at all to me or my son, didn't
come over to smell the baby, or greet me, or do anything different at
      all.
It just watched us moving around the house, so quiet
eventually running upstairs to hide in its crate
when the baby's cries were too loud.
I never even thought of petting the dog
never saw anyone else touch it, either, never could figure out

why my mother-in-law had brought it home.
I don't even remember it having a name.
A few months later, the dog was gone, and no one ever mentioned
what had happened to it, why it wasn't there any more
why it had even been there in the first place.
I remember walking around my mother-in-law's house
peering into side rooms, looking for the dog, the dog crate
some random squeaky toy, a gnawed-on rawhide bone,
anything belonging to a dog

but it was like there had never been a dog in the house at all.

Cul-de-Sac

You dig holes in me as though strip mining
was the most natural thing in the world in a marriage
exposing all of the layers of imperfect clay and silt and sand

beneath the false vestiges of bottomless topsoil. I bend beneath
your backhoe of logic and endless critiques, release the secrets and lies

that always kept me safe before, I am bare rock beneath you
I am small white pebbles ground smooth to nothing
beneath the onslaught of an ancient sea.

Retreat

I tell myself the robots won't be able to reach me
out here in the country, won't look for me
huddled beneath a milking cow in the morning,
one tin bucket beneath her teats
another over my head.

I tell myself the robocalls won't be able to find me out here
beneath the trees, they won't know
there's a slim window of two or three hours a day
that cell phone signals actually reach this place
won't know that I've covered all the roads leading here
in loose gravel and fake plants.

Summer

The June bug beats its wings
against the kitchen window, noisily whirring
as if trying to get in, or at least
get my attention. I open the oven, pull out
the roast I've been cooking, wonder what it is
the little beetle wants, why it panics so.

There are certain odors that attract insects, perhaps
there is something in the combination of beef and carrots
and sliced potatoes that makes a June bug think of love
or maybe it's the perfume I've put on tonight
or maybe its mate has been squished
under the stack of Goodwill-destined boxes I've been filling all day.
There's really no way to know.

I ladle the tender beef and vegetables onto my family's plates
think of the beetle watching us through the window
imagine the panic I'd feel myself if it were me,
standing outside some stranger's window
imagining I'd smelled my husband through a crack in the glass
lured in and taken by another woman
even one from another species.

Dismantling

The cannibals discover there are no flightless birds inside of me,
no tiny mice curled up in the dark, empty spaces, no fist-sized but-
terflies
with wings as strong and thick as bats',
none of the things I believed had been nestled in my chest

for too many years to count. They find my bones, also,
are indeed solid, there are none missing,
there is no specific physical imperfection to blame for
the things I always felt I was lacking.

Stripped of my skin, I could be any other woman
trapped behind glass at a local museum, propped up for display
in a pine coffin carefully and purposefully aged
with sponged-on black tea and crackle paint.

Waiting for the Wind

She's angry because she can't just dump the files out the window, can't
       let
50 years' of memory float down the street. Secretly, I agree with her
that all of the letters, the legal paperwork, the family photographs
should find their way into dark alleys and pools of gutter runoff
where the sloping forms of rats and raccoons can rip them into nests
make them the foundation of an actual happy home.

But the address she shared with my father for so many years
is on most of the paperwork, can be traced back to her
maybe incur a fine for littering. I point this out to her, remind her
she's been left too little to live on as it is, even less
if she has to go to court. She sighs and agrees,
replaces the papers clutched in her arms
carefully in the box they came out of, almost too carefully.
She's not going to get rid of them.

Years from now, angry myself, I will be the one standing at the open
       window
hands filled with copies of divorce papers that were never signed,
only reissued every few years
photographs of a happy family hiding terrible lies, will I have the
       strength
to shred all of this baggage, or will I merely tuck it away into yet
       another shoebox
offer it to my children as some sort of legacy, tell them
this is all that's left of a life?

The Plan

The flies crawl over the carcass in search of an opening: an eye, a
  gaping, damp nostril
some small abrasion or puncture wide enough to crawl into. They
  disappear, one by one
into the slowly-bloating body of the dead cow, deposit their eggs,
take to the air.

In days, the cow will come to life again, spotted skin wriggling and
  twitching
as eggs unfurl to release the maggots within, pushing at the confines
  of their home
as they stretch and contract, struggling for freedom.

Interactions in the Park

The tiny bird ruffles its feathers, flutters its wings
in a call-and-response game with the plastic bag in my hand.
I can't sing or whistle or chirp like the bird
but somehow, I can still communicate my appreciation
for his little dance in the tree.

Beneath the freeway overpass, blue-black grackles
erupt in a cacophony of car alarms and sirens
gleaned from years of nesting so close to so much traffic.
Sometimes, it's hard to appreciate nature
when it exerts itself this much
to celebrate us.

Geoffrey

He likes to play with dolls.
I keep finding pieces
of Barbie lying around the house,
plastic limbs
sprawled on the stairs, scalped beach bunnies
staring back at me, wide blue eyes
in the goldfish bowl
and floating in the toilet.
I've told him a million times
to pick up after himself
but it doesn't do any good.

He likes to play with dolls.
I keep hearing him
making up dialogues, both his and hers,
high-pitched girlish giggles
and screams from the bedroom
the dull scratch of garden tools
in the backyard
tiny mounds with Styrofoam
headstones appearing not
so mysteriously
overnight.

March

The first ants of the season are spilling out onto the sidewalk
Warmed by the unexpected sunshine. There are so many of them
They look like upturned earth, like someone took a stick
And carefully scraped dirt onto the sidewalk in a pile
So thickly spread you can't see the pavement beneath.

My daughter asks me if they're fire ants, wonders
If she would be stripped to the bone like a cow she saw on TV
If she stood in the middle of the pile and let them swarm over her.
I tell her no, but stay away anyway,
There's too many there to know for sure what they'll do.

The Funeral

We put the toaster in the paper boat, set it in the water. Predictably,
the paper boat collapses under the weight of the boxy toaster,
      crumples around it
like a flower at sunset, sinks to the stones lining the bottom of the
      lake.
It's hard to bury a toaster properly, pay homage to the service
a household appliance has given one's family for so many years.

Someday, when robots excavate the ruins of our homes, they'll
      wonder
at the ignoble way we discarded these appliances, gape at the savagery
of mobiles and windchimes made from blender blades and cake
      beaters
hypothesize about the significance of so many televisions and cell
      phones.
Perhaps they'll find our toaster, rusted solid after years of being
      submerged
marvel at the waste, wonder at the ceremony.

Caution Man

you are
caustic, sarcastic, silent picture black-caped villain
the open flame I worship, insectile
unable
to
fly
away

this is a sickness, my skin
sloughs off where you have damaged me
burn victim, beyond repair, rubber gloves
something you might have liked for dinner
once, too long ago

in the mausoleum's wings
feet always exit
stage right

you are
fetish, fantasy, enchanting fucking nutcase
people should stay away from me
some people
have tried
to help

you whisper of a place
where we will always be together
suburbia, cleaning products, postman, mace, a place
I still believe exists, Paradise?
let me have another look
remind me
why I hate you so much

Floating Away

I put the tiny boat
in the water and watch it
float away. Somewhere,
someday,

someone
will pull it out of the water,
either intact
or as a sodden, soggy newspaper mess, find

a tiny plastic bag
full of ashes
a sprig of dead lavender
your photograph, our wedding rings

and wonder

what it all means.

Now That You're Dead

parts of me remember your footsteps
on the stairs, parts of me
scream to forget
your hand on the door, your fingers
on my flesh, things
that never seemed to fit
quite right

I hear your feet dragging down
the same hallway, specter
sensing my room on a time-learned path
hollow fingers brush my hair
back from my forehead
shadows no longer ask
if I'm asleep

Uptown

The newspaper makes me angry and I prepare myself
for a day of punching Nazis. I read about the local museum
being infiltrated by white supremacists and so I plan my day
around a visit uptown. My daughter asks me where we're going and I
      tell her
we're going to fuck some shit up.

I keep my eyes peeled for guys with shaved heads and swastika pins
combat boots and iron crosses but I don't see any. Someone says
something kind of racist on the bus next to me and I look at them
but then they shut up as if they know what's in my head.

The Problem with Educational T.V.

The rat on t.v. has had the top of his head
removed, and his tiny pink brain
stabbed with colored wires. I recite Buddhist mantras
aloud, trying to coax the little creature
to join me, since someone once told me chanting
alleviates pain, and I imagine having your skull cut open
must be really painful.

Tiny whiskers quiver at me over hundreds of electronic
miles, and the stupid rat isn't chanting, doesn't realize
I'm trying to help, and suddenly
I have to go to the bathroom

but I can't leave the room, can't leave the television
because if I stopped watching this horrible show
for one moment

he'd be putting up with all this crap
for nothing.

Trying to Quit

naked, sharing a cigarette   we exchange
terrible lies   beneath these stained sheets
we mean something
stronger
than the definition   of these distorted love poems
I breathe   into your neck

I'm losing my mind with you   inside me
there are places in me
you can never go   memories   no
screaming to meet you no
slide over me   slick   onto me
take away
my dreams

The Decorating Preferences of Starlings and Housewives

The voices of frogs are coming in through the air conditioner vents
so loud in the rain it sounds like they're in here with us
perhaps hidden under the couch, or nestled in a comforter
clustered in a group of bright skin and gold eyes
watching us from the candy dish on the coffee table.

If it were up to me, the sinks would be overflowing with tadpoles
water lilies would sprout in the toilet, goldfish and catfish
would twist and turn in the bathtub. I would welcome otters and
      long-necked cranes
to my bedroom, move furniture aside to make room for them all.
But I have been told I can't do any of this.

The sparrows are chirping so loud in the bushes outside
it sounds like their voices are coming from inside the kitchen
      cupboards
that if I were to open the cabinet to get out a pot or pan
a flock of tiny brown birds would flutter out in dismay.
If it were up to me, finches could build nests in the rack meant for
      cookbooks
weave intricate baskets around the curtain rods for their young
fight for nesting rights in the breadbox, its bounty of stale bread
but I have been told that these things cannot happen
I have been told that this never will be.

Where We're Going

we rolled the windows up against the rain and my father
said "I wonder what that husband of yours
is doing right now" and I
just looked out through the streaky glass
and said nothing watching countryside

slide away in varying shades of green. behind me
the baby cried in his car seat tired
of being strapped down for six hours straight
and I wanted to cry but grown-ups don't do that. outside the car

cornstalks unfolded under the onslaught of rain
sparse trees danced in waves of rippling light
and everything I thought I knew
about where I was going
and who I was going to be

faded into a black spot behind us
a black spot of nothing against a straight line of horizon.

Moving Day

The old house slides past the windows, disappears
in the rearview mirror, turns the corner
and it's gone, that whole part of our lives together
in that place, the backyard where I carried my baby around each
       night,
waiting for him to be able to see
the millions of stars suddenly visible on stark winter nights,
the stunted flowers I grew from cheap seed packets, the way

the baby clothes fluttered on the laundry line
printed with bright-colored cartoon monkeys and puppy dogs.
He sleeps between us in the front seat, so quiet, unaware
that he will never see that back yard again, that he will never see
the children from this neighborhood again.

There are so many miles ahead of us, so many miles
of empty, unfamiliar country, flat, yellow plains, small, unfriendly
       towns
rest stops full of hollow-eyed people and old people
who ask too many questions, concrete cities where flowers rarely
       bloom
and the residents only come outside at night. Three thousand miles
to hold onto and believe in
promises of white beaches, seabirds, and no more snow
almost seems like too much to ask.

Shopping Trip

He asks if I'm okay because my shopping list
is nothing but razors. I tell him I'm fine, take the list
write "disco ball" at the very top, and now
everything's fine. There's nothing to see here.

The only windows in my room are the ones
I've drawn myself. There are mountains
in those landscapes, far-off places that only exist
in my dreams. When he comes back from the store

everything will be fine.

Now

My boots slip on the ice and I struggle to stay standing
and think, "This? Is this how I die? On a sidewalk
some idiot neighbor forgot to shovel, taking the dog out for a walk?"
And I don't fall but I still wonder if I'll make it home
or if I'll slip somewhere else, die on my back
the dog watching me with concern but too well-trained
to bark or run away.

I come and he comes and my heart pounds against my chest
and I wonder, "Now? If this how I'll go?
too old to fuck properly without worrying about death?"
And even after my body settles into the warmth before sleep
I'm still worrying about how I'll be found
dead in the morning, skin pale and drawn,
jaw sagging next to a puddle of drool
I'm already sorry for whoever finds me first.

Hands Fall Like Dying Butterflies

Let's call this love: the waves folding over your head
like the wings of a tent flap, the suffocating confines
of warm blankets in a morning you don't remember entering
the heavy arm of a stranger thrown over your chest that won't let you
   go.
This, let's call this last breath: home, the sinking resignation

of concrete boots pulling you across the threshold into the kitchen
the anchors that tie you to the stove, the ballast bags of screaming
   children
that know who you are and why you're here
even if you don't. Here, this place you belong

we'll draw a circle around it on the map
so you know where you're supposed to be, a tiny point engulfed
in winged possibility that you will never know, those dreams
will not be allowed to hatch.
There are alarms set to different times all through this house
and your feet know when and where to take you to answer them all.

Genesis

We'll just assume it was all construed by men in suits
pointing at scrawled-over blackboards with long wooden sticks, we'll assume
they knew what they were doing because men in suits
always claim responsibility for these things.
There is always a plan and a chain of command.

Let's pretend that there were no women yet, that these men
who created the universe could also make their own tea
take their own notes, and were truly responsible for all of their claims
and that this cruel joke that keeps women hidden in the shadows
as great things happen around them, completely excludes them
was something that happened overnight, an accident
some side effect of the universe exploding.

Surma

we identify each other
by our ceremonial tattoos
ritualistic burnings—in the dark
I feel the spot where someone dared you
to put a cigarette out
your fingers brush the jagged "x"
that was supposed to stop my breath

anthropologists, we explore
each other's damaged pasts
the keloid I got in ninth grade
making happy faces with a lighter, the circle of blue dots
a twelve-year-old did with a safety pin and India ink
the Braille graffiti of your chest
ribs shattered and warped, a mangled child
and a drunk stepfather—we are never

completely naked

Where the Trembling Comes in

I've taken to sleeping naked at night
sprawled out on the floor for invisible cameramen
eyes rolled back, all the way back in my head
imagining the feel of rough police hands
as they trace me in chalk, another
tragic casualty and I've

taken to writing suicide notes
practicing my handwriting, where the trembling comes in
who to single out for love and for blame
and who to leave out, blatantly

and I've taken to stealing strange men's clothes
snuck out of the wash at the public laundry
to scatter about and around my bedroom
like a parade of cruel lovers, all of them

just passing through.

After the Funeral

it's become a contest of who knew first
who first found out how and when he or she died
who was closest, who has the best story. we get ugly
in our nostalgia, tread a difficult balance between
preserving the subject's sudden sainthood
while expunging our most pointed, painful, awful memories
find some way to say we should have seen it coming
express surprise that it took so long.

afterwards, we each retreat to our private musings
on how if things had been different
it could have been any one of us
it should have been someone else. there's a dark, uncertain target
over everyone we know now, ready to move on
who will be next.

Saint Joan

The cold of my church's stone
climbs through my feet, unnoticed
an unrecognized saint
with a spike taped to the inside of my arm
missing the holes between my fingers
slow revelations, Zoroastic fire
burns thick in metal trashcans
light is good,
dark is evil
there is nothing else.

There is no voice for the New Word
my tongue
flops helpless against my parched lips, habit
curls the muscles back
I preach
in puke. The relic
falls from my hands, brown still bubbling
in its womb
as I lean back and watch the evil recede
as the Holy Spirit enters the room.

I walk among the catacombs of the city
beneath the blind ziggurat skyscrapers
the muezzin's post long abandoned
faith replaced by electronic eyes. Graffiti speaks
New Christian to me, in aerosol paint
on the sides of the subway cars as they rattle past
the entrance of my home, spreading the faith.

The Day the Leaves Started to Change

The bird flutters into the church like some sort of portent
disturbs the service with a flurry of feathers. It would be nice
if it was a dove, or some brilliant, golden, phoenix-type of bird
but it's just a sparrow come in from the cold.

The preacher waits until the bird has settled before continuing on
with his speech, but he is distracted. Every time the bird
moves to another corner of the church, he instinctively covers the top
of his bald head with one robed arm as if
too used to having birds shit on him

while flying overhead.

Topiary

children wander through
the courtyards
mindless of the darkness
stimuli-starved minds
slaver at their passage

like bats released from
secret holes
their robes enfold their
tiny guests
swiftly sliding back to the
candlelit altars

the flowers of the
monastery
wither under the burden
of secrets God
has forgiven

Your Hand in Mine

The sun shines brightly as your voice
is still in the air, subtle constant
a warning echo of your passage. That day
smiling at somewhere
is a photograph of me.

Leaves appear on trees as conversations
slowly unfold green between us
as timorous as field mouse paws
resting delicately on plastic garbage bags
filled with possibility.

I long to face this spring dead-on, reconstruct
these last death throes of love
as anything but.

Knee-High in the Weeds

The doctor laughs when I tell her my plan
was to give birth in the back yard, like my cat did her kittens
that it just felt like the safest place to me right now.
She says she doesn't do house calls, so I'll have to see her here.

I regret the touch of cold metal against my skin, all of the poking and
   prodding
the ultrasound that shows only the skeleton of the human child inside
   me.
I wanted so much for there to be a litter of kittens, and I tell the
   doctor this
and she laughs again and tells me only cats have kittens, my baby
   looks fine.

At home, I am angry that so many things I say these days
are making people laugh, because I don't mean them to be funny, I
   don't.
I tell the baby inside me that most people don't take me seriously
and to not be surprised at the stories people will tell.

Wheelchair

avoiding eyes he pushes and
pulls himself to the edge
of the railing to stare
fascinated
at the beautiful woman performing
incredible acts of agility and
strength on the ever-so-steady back
of the prancing white pony
stares
convinced that if he
could only catch her eye and
distract her or maybe frighten
her delicate mount she'd stumble
and fall and they'd take
her away only to find
that she would never walk
again
and she'd cry and all
of her friends would gather
quietly
around her hospital bed
offer inane words of encouragement
then quickly walk out
of her life and then
he would
push and pull his way
into the hospital and to
the side of her bed
and let her know that
she would never
have to be alone

Unfurling

The dust finally settles, and it's safe to come out.
Doors of fallout shelters creak open,
exhale recycled air and the smell
of confinement. The first step
cautiously out into the open.

Huddled masses stretch themselves into the halls
of new palaces: abandoned, themed McDonald's
massive stock exchange buildings bearing reliefs of
extinct flowers and grains
an ice skating rink, big enough
for children and horses.

Self-proclaimed kings and queens
spontaneously create new religions
and traditions, declare them in a competition of cacophony
through broken skyscraper windows
and flimsy observation decks
littered with the bodies of sparrows and pigeons.

Rejection

you reek of cracked pots, conceptual pieces
method actors and evangelical chalk
promise circulating clusters of black waves
gift-wrapped bluebirds
self-preservation.
show me a view of someone
else.

you are duct-taped unrecognizable
except for shouted orders
where I
can complete you
you are all sirens and flashing lights
and I can't understand
a word you're saying.

Woman Hiding from Her Husband as He Tries to Fix Her Brakeline

makes a story for the rain,
holds her hands over her
ears, allows her eyes to glaze as
sunlight fades away, she

makes excuses for the
storm, hides her head beneath the
dirt, pretends to sleep, deaf
to the crashing sounds, she

waits, inside, cautious of
the returning storm, creeps outside
slow at noon, picks up the

beer cans.

Hospice

Caught in the snare of She'ol, dew gives brief life to dust
as they pull the tubes loose, hand me a bag of pills.
In the wake of disaster, we drive home from the hospital.

I dissect the memories for her, one last time
alphabetize faces in stacks of photographs
with the passionless objectivity of a grunt laborer
excavating layers of ash-buried Pompeii. I dissect the memories for
     her

as they come, unbidden, help catalogue
and file our stories away impartially as
a lab tech methodically filling slides with samples of cancer, she
mutters, "so that's where we went wrong"
too many times for comfort.

The Mannequin's Last Stop

her arms break off and the waves take them away
roll them down the beach over and over until they're gone.
I wonder what the seals and dolphins will think
when they see those white, disembodied hands

reaching out to them from the depths, if they'll recognize them
as having belonged to some facsimile of a human
some amusement to frighten each other with, build ghost stories
       around
or they'll confuse them for some new type of coral
some new construction project perhaps not yet finished.

Eventually, lesser sea creatures will seek out the ceramic limbs,
scallops and limpets will bind their shells
to the insides of worn elbow joints, while anemones and sea stars
and velvet-black sea slugs will make new homes in the holes and pits
made by careless forklift tines and clumsy delivery men.

Time Left Over

I wear my mother's winter coat, reflect
on the life she never had—sacrifice
the father that wasn't ghost hand in mine
sixteen years old and so much in love so

flamboyant, faded photos on the mantle
a smile I never saw, collapsing seduction
fading into the gray woman who held me
and cried. And now I'm her, wearing

her clothes and fighting against natural
reorientation. I remember growing old
growing up in her my house, lawnmower
squealing banging in my head, echoing father's

private mantra. It's easy to forgive
terror him of what he did to me
us both this one—thank god
there isn't a gun in this house.

How I Spent My Summer Vacation

Pull out the specimen drawer
see how I spent my summer vacation.
I have been chasing butterflies from sunup to sundown
hands full of pins and cardboard mounts
covered in silvery dust from careless blunders.

When I put away my jacket for the night, my pockets
are taped up tight, sealed against any intruders lured
by the scent of flailing wings or accidental bloodletting.
Spiders follow me around the house, as if
they can sense the carnage clinging to me.

Reflux

time leaches the color from
holding-hands photographs and I
see myself dying
in the backs of polished spoons.
memories of a childhood love will only
be that: memories. I can hear the earth stop
in the complete quiet that follows
speaking your name out loud.

you have pulled your roots out of me
so completely
I don't know where to find the wounds
I'm dying from
I don't know how to heal.
you are everything but summer to me
and now even the warm parts of the day
can't protect me from memories of
half-spoken promises
too-real dreams.

Bank Managers at the Zoo

it's hard to picture
those clean, stocky women with
short brown hair
it's hard to picture them
naked in bed, belly swollen
criss-crossing purple veins
it's hard to picture them
screaming in birth, legs spread

bowels loosing over paper sheets
as the head breaks through
it's hard to picture them
reaching out to voluntarily hold something
as messy and sticky as a newborn infant
while the doctor coaxes out afterbirth
closes incisions with thread
it's hard to picture them

being anything but professional
and detached from a world
of sweat and saliva and animal sex
to think of them as earthy, human
just another woman, someone like me

The Wolf

she hungers
from behind the stacks of boulders
crated in from her
original home, the mismatched groves
of pine and oak
that never quite smell
like they belong to the ground.

she waits
for the zoo to close for the night, for the crowds
of curious children, mothers with infants
men
to go home, taking with them
the longings that will never be met
pretending to be content with just
howling, alone, at the moon.

Today

wheels clack and crash and bang and smash as it
roars down the tracks, boxcars and bright lights
and splintering wood and spray-painted metal
the rush of the wind sucking everything into
its wake a dragon a monster
my bright-eyed salvation

oh, the whirr of noisy metal wheels as I choose my spot
on the landing, the widening eyes
of the people to the right of me
the people to the left of me
as they realize what I mean to do
this is happening today.

Some of the Things that Happen Around Us

The violinist folds himself into his case, tucks his wings
in carefully, folds his arms across his chest, sleeps.
Beside his case is a smaller case, with a handle, and in it
his violin also rests, perhaps dreaming of new strings.

There is no need for furniture in this house. Everything sits or sleeps
in a case or a cage. The shelves are filled with kennels containing
sleeping cats and dogs, covered birdcages of canaries and finches
parrots who think they're in charge. Even the unnecessary couch is
covered

encased in clear plastic, as if being preserved for freshness
as though some day, the violinist might have company
and they will want something brand new to sit on.

Self Portrait

My daughter spreads the glue over the board
and picks out the colors and sizes of the seeds. Together,
we carefully trickle waves of millet and poppy next to each other
draw out the outline of the farmhouse with such slow, steady, patient
        hands
it's almost as though a pair of strangers are drawing the picture
instead of us. My daughter takes deep, slow breaths
as though she's afraid that normal breathing will disrupt her
preternaturally straight lines, and as I listen to her breathing, I realize
I've been holding my own breath completely.

My daughter squirts another careful blob of glue onto the plywood
and this time, haystacks blossom under a stream of flat yellow gourd
        seeds.
For a moment, they look so real I have to stop and step back from the
        picture
take it all in. My daughter continues to work as I watch,
drawing the outlines of fields with tiny green split peas and dried
        zinnia seeds
filling in the gaps with handfuls of lettuce seeds so tiny they look like
        sand
somehow brought to our dusty farm from a beach an impossible
        world away.

Never Was

There was a baby that should have been born
before me, it was the baby
that made my father marry my mother
the baby that trapped them together.
The baby disappeared soon after the wedding
lost in the inconsolable melancholy
that never left my mother's eyes.

I used to imagine what it would have been like
to have had that older brother or sister
around, if it would have made me stronger
having an older sibling to protect me
if my parents would have been happier
if there had been two of us, not just me.

You with the Sparrow

descending over barren hills, as if
we had a destination, rain falling
from our hair—a theory of the sun-scorched

our fingertips, borders between states disappearing
like sacred ash in a smoldering iron pot. You
laughed at my excitement, our mutual relief at

a final escape. Numbers of gees flew
overhead, flying south, back towards Louisiana
could hear them singing the blues. Their feathers taunted us

our slow, tired bondage to Earth—we talked of
handcuffing ourselves to chickens and doves
as a solution to all problems. It itched my tired, troubled sparrow

ache for a little while. Crossing final
flat, golden plains we dreamed aloud of our future,
a vegetable garden—the flocks thinned

as the sun went down, great
clouds of birds came to rest
we passed them in our car.

Halcyon

I dreamed I was a fireman. With an axe.
You were on fire.

I dreamed I was a plumber. Just here to patch a leak.
Stopped the water pouring out of your fishbowl prison.

I dreamed I was the governor of the state of Indiana.
I was in the shower, singing "Figarofigarofigaro" at the top of my
       lungs.
The electrocutioner shakes his head at you, sadly hanging up the
       phone.

I dreamed I was a barber. In San Francisco. My office was near the
top of one of the only
skyscrapers in town. I had just received a disturbing phone call:
my mother had been arrested for shoplifting.
I felt the tremors begin in my hands, through the floor.
You insisted I use the straight razor
to trim the stubble roughing your neck.

Don't Try This at Home

(for Alex, the guy who used to live in my grandparents' basement apartment I never got to meet him in person but he had a real cool car he always parked on the lawn and I always wondered what he was like)

Scene One
Somehow I get my gun out before
he does and I pull the hammer back
s l o w l y take aim and   see, now,
I hate this. My thumb is always so
goddamn
sweaty I'm afraid
the hammer's gonna slip before it's fully cocked
the gun's gonna go off before

Scene Two
hello I thought it would be funny to put a full bag of manure on your porch and set it on fire   I have planned this for days   it would have to be in the morning for only in the morning would you think stomping out a fire on the front porch in your slippers would be the smart thing to do how the Hell was I supposed to know those swank wool smoking slippers were so f l a m m a b l e and your robe and the little spot of dried shaving cream on your face and that black shit you put in your hair every night that stinks so much I have to go home to sleep because I'm afraid I'll accidentally roll too close to you and puke all over the bed

Scene Three
okay, someone is definitely following me you should
NEVER duck into an alley when being pursued.
That's what all the stupid girls do.
I have a gun and I will walk out in the open.
I have a gun and I will walk out in the open naked and stop, naked,
under the streetlight, where everyoneanyoneyou and see me naked

HEY
do you see me, motherfucker?
Come and get me.
look, I'm naked

Scene Four
A priest walks into a bar.
A clown with an invisible dog walks into a bar.
A psychopath with an axe walks into a bar.
I stand outside the bar, a can of lighter fluid at my feet
here is your salvation. I can show you a way out
of the building without using a door CAN YOU SEE ME NOW?
are you listening?
Say something romantic or I will kill you.

OTHER ANAPHORA LITERARY PRESS TITLES

The History of British and American Author-Publishers
By: Anna Faktorovich

Notes for Further Research
By: Molly Kirschner

The Encyclopedic Philosophy of Michel Serres
By: Keith Moser

The Visit
By: Michael G. Casey

How to Be Happy
By: C. J. Jos

A Dying Breed
By: Scott Duff

Love in the Cretaceous
By: Howard W. Robertson

The Second of Seven
By: Jeremie Guy

Lightning Source UK Ltd.
Milton Keynes UK
UKHW011434120620
364910UK00002B/361